PANZERWAFFE AT WAR
(1) NUREMBERG TO MOSCOW

Text by Robert Michulec & Thomas Anderson
Color plates by Wojciech Kloński

CONCORD
PUBLICATIONS COMPANY

Pre War Development

The history of Germany´s armored force, the *Panzerwaffe*, can only be described as amazing. When, at the beginning of World War Two, Poland was invaded in a mere three weeks, France, the United Kingdom and many other nations were shocked. The success of this young branch of service was so overwhelming that any resistance was swept away. German terms like *Panzer* and *Blitzkrieg* became common in many other languages.

It is not easy to understand this dynamic period of history. More than any other nation, Germany understood the tactical and strategical rules of World War One, and the true nature of armored cars and tanks. More than any other politicians, the Nazis broke with their own military establishment, consequently rejecting obsolete traditions. The cavalry was dismounted to a great extent, its organizational structure being partly used for the new tank force. The old-fashioned infantry was regarded as of secondary importance, its equipment not being modernized to the same extent as that of the tank divisions. The tanks, with their firepower, armor protection, and stunning mobility, were the outriders of a new age.

After World War One the Treaty of Versailles imposed severe restrictions on the nation of Germany. Its army was especially affected. The number of soldiers was limited to 100,000 men, and any development of modern military technology was forbidden. Germany could not have control of aircraft, tanks and chemical agents - in the final analysis, the three technical means that helped to decide the outcome of World War One. An interallied control commission supervised the disarmament of Germany, and the German war industry was forced to stop any research and production in Germany. As a consequence, essential parts of this research were evacuated abroad. These restrictions, justified or not, were never accepted by the general population or any government in Germany.

Bourgeois and nationalist, as well as liberal, groups fought against the *Schandvertrag* - the "treaty of shame" - of Versailles. They created the legend of the *Dolchstoß*, the stab in the back, which overthrew an undefeated and heroic army. This ubiquitous tale of an isolated nation´s righteous struggle against an almighty alliance of enemies was one reason behind the unquestioned course of history that Germany would take. Economic decline and growing unemployment, two serious problems that plagued Germany in the 1930s, joined with this obscure feeling of lost honor, forming the ideal hotbed for radical thought. Adolf Hitler´s seizure of power waited at the end of a string of straightforward, yet avoidable developments.

The development of new tools of war, particularly tanks and artillery, had to proceed in secrecy, but an ally was found in the East. The young Soviet Union had to reorganize their armed forces when their five-million-man civil war army was demobilized in 1920. After three years of revolution and counter-revolution, Russia desperately needed support in establishing a military doctrine and help in forming an effective military instrument. Germany had everything the Soviets were looking for: knowledge, experience and a sophisticated armament industry. On the other hand, the vastness of Russia offered Germany the ability to develop weapons far away from any control. Germany profited by this cooperation to a much larger extent than the Soviet Union. In early 1920, the German aircraft manufacturer Junkers established a production site near Moscow, and a chemical company planned large-scale production of the war gas Lost. Apart from these enterprises, the secret *Fliegergruppe* (pilot group) established a testing and training site in Lipeck. All goals, both in technical and personnel respects, were reached. By 1933, 120 fighter pilots and 100 airmen, the cadre of what would become the *Luftwaffe*, had been trained.

From 1927 on, the Reichswehr operated a tank school at Kama near Kazan. Here the first developments of Krupp and Rheinmetall were tested, disguised as farming tractors. The 18-ton *Großtraktor* (heavy tractor, of which three different prototypes were sent to Kama by Daimler, Krupp and Rheinmetall) featured a large hull with a WWI-style rotary track. Armament consisted of a short-barreled 7.5cm gun in a small turret. A small rear turret carried a machine gun. These early developments were similar to tank designs of other nations — Vickers Independent (U.K.), Char 2C (France) and heavy tanks M-1 and M-2 (Soviet Union). All these vehicles featured one main and one or more auxiliary turrets.

At the same time, the *Leichtertraktor* (light tractor) was produced to supplement the heavy breakthrough tanks. This 9-ton tank was to go into production in different versions, such as supply vehicle, weapons carrier and light tank. Similar in appearance to the Vickers Medium Tank Mk II, it featured a half-automatic 3.7cm gun under light armor.

Neither the *Großtraktor* nor the *Leichtertraktor* proved to be successful. The Germans faced many technical problems: the transmission was a weak point with all designs, and the engines were not stable under the adverse conditions suffered by tanks. The tracks were especially prone to damage. However, it must be said that thanks to the Kama tank school, German industry gained tremendous technological knowledge in the field of armored vehicles. The cooperation was ended on the German side in late 1933, a few months after Hitler´s seizure of power. Although the two nations never entered into an official military treaty, they cooperated in military-technical development for more than ten years. As for Germany, the first mass-production tank left the production lines in 1934. This would have been impossible without Kama!

Starting in 1932, two tank designs entered production. The 23-ton *Neubaufahrzeug*, principally derived from the *Großtraktor*, was designed one main and two auxiliary turrets. After five of these breakthrough tanks left Rheinmetall´s factory, production was stopped. This was partly due to economical reasons and partly due to the fact that the *Reichswehr* leadership preferred a single-turret design. The other tank was a light 5-ton vehicle built by Krupp. Produced under the designation "LAS", for *Landwirtschaftlicher Ackerschlepper* (agricultural tractor), this vehicle featured a design that was typical of all further German tank developments. The engine was located at the rear, and drive was provided via a front transmission. This arrangement resulted in a comparatively high protection level for the driver, as the transmission block stopped or absorbed the impact of a penetrating shell. The frontal drive sprocket affected a good self-cleaning of the tracks, a fact not unimportant in the early 1930s. The "LAS" was adopted for mass production, with 477 units of the initial version (Ausf. A) being delivered between 1933 and 1934.

First Action of the Panzerwaffe

It can be assumed that as early as 1935, shortly after his "appointment" to the post of Chancellor, Hitler planned an expansion of Germany´s sphere of influence. However, the instruments for carrying out his military plans were still being developed. The military organization was still in its infancy, and the men of the young air and tank force were untrained. Hitler found an ideal training ground for his armed forces in Spain, where a bloody civil war took place between 1936 and 1939. Hitler, along with Italy´s leader, Mussolini, supported the nationalist Spaniards under General Franco. Germany´s help consisted of some 200 tanks (Pz.Kpfw. I Ausf. A and Ausf. B) and tactical and technical assistance. Italy provided about 250 tankettes (CV3/33 and CV3/35). The people´s front government, on the opposing side, received 362 tanks — mainly T-26s — from the Soviet Union.

The German military learned a number of lessons from this first action:

1. Their combat tactics proved to be basically adequate. Tank attacks can only be successful within the framework of a divison´s combined weapons.

2. The choice of the appropriate assault tactic is decisive.

3. The Pz.Kpfw. I proved to be no match for the T-26, so large-scale production of tanks with stronger armarment and armor was demanded.

In general, these lessons were accepted and further developed by the Germans. German industry, however, was not able to produce the desired quantities.

In 1938 Hitler annexed the western part of Czechoslovakia, then one year later gave the order to occupy the eastern part as well. This coup, tolerated by a Franco-British appeasement policy, strengthened the German arsenal significantly with the complete equipment of 36 divisions. Among these weapons were 218 Pz.Kpfw. 35(t)s and 98 Pz.Kpfw. 38(t)s, which were modern battle tanks with effective weapons by 1939 standards.

Hitler´s aggressive policy resulted in an expansion of the German sphere of influence in all of Europe. The first victim, however, was the young republic of Poland. The German assault of Poland came as a surprise on the 1st of September 1939. The bulk of the army was made up of 2,600 Pz.Kpfw. I and II tanks, both of which had limited combat value. Of the Pz.Kpfw. IIIs, designed as a main battle tank for tank vs. tank battles, only 98 reached the Panzer divisions. Armed with a 3.7cm gun and protected by 30mm armor, this vehicle was the strongest weapon of Germany´s arsenal. This low number of Pz. Kpfw IIIs clearly shows just how important the Czech vehicles really were. A further 211 Pz.Kpfw. IVs, with a short-barreled 7.5cm gun and very thin armor of 14.5mm, served as support tanks.

The Polish Army fielded 130 7-TP tanks, many of which were armed with a 37mm Bofors gun. The tank force was reinforced by 49 heavily armored French R-35 tanks. The rest of the tank force consisted of about 500 TK and TKS tankettes. This comparison of armored vehicles clearly shows that the German force was much stronger than the Polish. But more important than the total number or actual fighting power was the new strategy of combined weapons. The Luftwaffe attacked targets of strategic importance right from the beginning. Among these targets were 33 airfields, so the bulk of the Polish Air Force was as good as nailed to the ground. This was the hour of the dive-bombers, the Stukas. In close cooperation with the ground troops, the Luftwaffe attacked troop concentrations, baggage trains and artillery positions. The Panzer divisions, although not perfectly equipped, performed with deadly precision. A mere three days later, four Polish divisions were encircled and another one annihilated. The success took its toll, however. By the 4th of September the German formations had lost about 100 armored vehicles just in the northern districts. But the Polish losses were much higher. On 6th September, the XVI.Panzerkorps reached the outskirts of Warsaw. The city surrendered on the 28th, and a few days later the last fighting ended.

The invasion of Poland, often called the "18-day campaign", confirmed the lessons learned in Spain:

1. The combined advance of tanks and infantry, supported by artillery and Luftwaffe units, proved to be successful in large-scale operations. The concentration of tanks breaking through the enemy lines at points of tactical or strategical importance could decide the battle.

2. The armor and weaponry of German tanks was not satisfactory, especially on the lighter tanks. The heavier Pz.Kpfw. IIIs and IVs were also vulnarable to 37mm fire. Suspensions and transmissions were prone to damage, and losses were comparatively high.

3. German industrial capacity was not sufficient to provide the Panzer divisions with larger numbers of heavy tanks (Pz.Kpfw. III and IV). In fact, the cheap Pz.Kpfw. I was introduced only because of this inability.

In summary, it was the German tactics and fighting morale, but not the weaponry, that decided the Polish campaign. The Anglo-French appeasement policy had completely failed, and Great Britain and France had little choice but to enter the war. But neither nation did anything to relieve or help Poland.

Shortly after the Polish campaign was decided, the German troops were regrouped because an attack on Germany's Western Front was anticipated. But the governments of France and Great Britain hesitated. The memory of World War One was still vivid, and nobody wanted another Great War. France, as the most likely objective on Germany's Western Front, relied on the Maginot Line, a complex of fortresses and pillboxes. The French felt safe behind this line, but since it was not yet completed, their military strategy in the event of a German assault contemplated a counterattack through the northern parts of Belgium. The center of the Franco-German border, however, was secured by the Ardennes, a large forest region that was believed to be impassable by armored formations.

While the western Allies were alarmed, aside from lodging formal protests, they took no action. In 1940, France had a large tank force. Together with the British Expeditionary Force, about 3,400 French tanks could be fielded, among them many heavy tanks with strong armor and armament. Good examples were the Char B1 bis heavy and the Somua S-35 medium tanks. The French 47mm antitank gun was one of the best available, penetrating 36mm at a range of 1,500 meters (1,640 yds). It should be remembered that at this time the strongest German tank, the Pz.Kpfw. III, had a maximum frontal armor of 30mm. In fact, the French Army was superior to the German, both in quality and quantity. The German Luftwaffe, however, had a decisive advantage.

As the year changed from 1939 to 1940, France suffered the fate of many democracies. While the government tried to reinforce the border troops and ordered a maximum output of war material, the communist party fought in the underground against these efforts. Four thousand highly specialized workers refused to produce desperately needed Melenit (a component of gun powder) because of a rumor that they would lose their hair in the process. In the arsenal of Montlucon, 120 antitank guns were destroyed due to sabotage. The situation in England was similar. Due to public laws, only unmarried men could be called to arms, and the trade unions prevented the extension of the daily work shift, which should have been implemented in time of war.

The next logical step for Germany to take in Hitler's war was to keep its back protected. The *Unternehmen Weserübung* — the occupation of Northern Europe — began on the 7th of April 1940. Denmark was invaded within one day, complying with this fate under protest. Norway was attacked from the seaside, and Oslo was taken by paratroopers and ground forces. Despite the intervention of English, French and Polish forces, Norway was forced to capitulate on the 10th of June.

The next German attack came on the 10th of May 1940. This day saw the first large scale action by paratroopers. Thousands of them jumped into the Dutch cities of Rotterdam and Den Haag and at the bridge of Moerdijk. Thus, a defense of the borders was rendered impossible, and the Dutch forces faced attacks from two sides. Although a number of strongpoints could be held, the invasion coud not be avoided.

Belgium suffered the same fate. The assault came so surprisingly and was so rapid that the defenders were not able to destroy the many bridges at the border. The mighty fortress Eben-Emael was paralyzed; German special forces destroyed all observation and artillery positions by shaped charges in a mere 17 minutes. The defense position, which should have stopped the aggressor for at least one week, was taken in a forenoon. The Belgian Army retreated to a defense line further to the west where, it was hoped, the Western allies could support the defense; a concentrated counterattack could then sweep back the German forces. The French had sent crack divisions to hold the line Breda-Dinont. The Ardennes were regarded as secure.

This was exactly what von Manstein had expected. Now, between the 13th and 15th of May, a strong force penetrated the MLR at Sedan. Generals Rommel and Guderian forced their way to the canal. The French 9th Army was annihilated, and despite a locally successful counterattack by De Gaulle´s tanks, the German troops reached Abbeville on the 20th of May. The French 1st Army and much of the BEF were cut off. A fortnight later the disaster of Dunkirk would follow — 40,000 French soldiers were captured and 340,000 were evacuated to England. All military equipment had to be left on the continent.

General Weygand used the time to establish a new defense line north of Paris. However, the French Army and the remnants of the BEF had lost all confidence in their abilities and their military leadership. The end was unavoidable. On the 22nd of June the armstice negotiations began; France, *La Grande Nation*, was defeated.

The reasons for the success of the German aggressor were manifold. Both the French Army and the BEF were unfit for a modern war. The strategical possibilities of armed forces were not realized. The German armored formations were used very flexibly, breaking through the defense lines like an armored wedge. The tanks advanced seperately from the infantry, which too often could not follow this impetus (for this reason Rommel was often criticized and called back). Behind the enemy lines they spread out and attacked from the rear or fought the French support and logistic units. The tactical side was similar. The high degree of communication during the battle allowed for very effective leadership. Local success was communicated immediately, and reinforcements could be called off in a very short time.

The complete German air superiority inflicted heavy losses in the hinterland; advancing troops, troop transports, lines of supply, and the railway´s system were attacked and destroyed.

The *Fall Gelb* — the invasion of France — was thoroughly analyzed by German military leaders. Although the Panzerwaffe had performed well, it was in a critical phase due to the following:

1. Armor protection of all German tanks was far too weak to withstand fire from enemy antitank guns or tanks. The Pz.Kpfw. III, designed for tank vs. tank engagements, had only 30 mm frontal armor.

2. Armament was regarded as ineffective. Neither the 3.7cm gun of the Pz.Kpfw. III nor the short-barreled 7.5cm gun of the Pz.Kpfw. IV could successfully defeat the heavily armed French tanks.

The Balkan Campaign

On the 26th of October 1940, the German Army began to regroup for Operation "Barbarossa", the planned invasion of the Soviet Union. Two days later, however, this regrouping was interrupted by the Italian attack against Greece. The Italian forces, badly led and equipped, were repulsed almost immediately. Hitler decided to launch a relief attack through Bulgaria and Romania, but the military coup in Belgrade on the 27th of March thwarted this plan. Now Hitler ordered his armies to attack both Yugoslavia and Greece.

In the morning of the 6th of April, fifteen divisions crossed the Yugoslavian border, and another nine attacked Greece. The campaign was quickly successful. After only three days the Metaxas line was penetrated, and on the 12th of April Belgrade was taken. At the end of April the fighting was over, and another Blitzkrieg came to an end. Operation "Marita" had shown that armored units could be used just as effectively under difficult geographic conditions. The mastering of the immense distances took a greater toll on men and materiel than the actual fighting. Once again the performance of the Panzerwaffe was analyzed and conclusions drawn:

1. Armored formations can be used successfully under complicated geographical conditions.

2. Tanks and armored vehicles had to face extraordinary stress during the Balkan campaign. The Pz.Kpfw. I and II showed heavy wear to their running gear systems, and damaged leaf springs and running wheels often led to the loss of the vehicle. The Pz.Kpfw. III and IV suffered from shredded rubber linings on their running wheels.

3. The weaponry and armor protection of the German tanks were sufficient in the Balkans since the Panzerwaffe faced relatively weak resistance from British and Greek armored units.

The invasion of Yugoslavia and Greece produced one critical side effect, however: Operation "Barbarossa" had to be postponed for five decisive weeks.

North Africa - The Birth of the Afrika Korps

At the beginning of 1941 the situation for the Italian forces in North Africa reached a critical phase. The British had overrun all of their positions, destroying two divisions. On the 22nd of January Tobruk was forced to capitulate. When, at the end of January, the whole of Cyrenaica was lost, Hitler ordered German troops under the command of General Erwin Rommel to intervene. The first units of the 5.leichte-Division landed in Tobruk on the 15th. In March, a limited reconnaissance raid expanded into a full-scale offensive by General Rommel. This attack surprised the British, and forced them back to Tobruk. But as early as mid-1941 Rommel was experiencing a weakness in the Afrika Korps - an unreliable and insufficient supply of men, weapons and ammunition. After the sinking of several German supply convoys by the Royal Navy, Rommel was forced to stop his offensive. In mid-November the British launched the Operation "Crusader" offensive. By the end of 1941, the Afrika Korps had been driven back to Benghazi and El Agheila.

For the Panzerwaffe, the following problems emerged:

1. The extreme climate had a disastrous effect on the German tanks. Dust destroyed weapons and engines, overburdened the air filters and bearings, and impaired the optics. Manufacturing firms in Germany immediately had to improve complete components. Most problems could be solved within a mere three months, though.

2. The Pz.Kpfw. I and II tanks reached the end of their service life as main battle tanks. Due to their weak armor protection and weaponry, they were used only for recconnaissance or protective duties.

3. To a large degree, the Pz.Kpfw. III was already armed with the 5cm L/42 KwK. Although better than the 3.7cm gun, this gun still was ineffective against the British infantry tanks. The Matilda or Valentine tank could be dealt with only at distances under 500 meters (540 yards). A stronger gun was needed. The Pz.Kpfw. IV's 7.5cm gun was inadequate as well since it lacked accuracy.

Operation "Barbarossa" - The Invasion of the Soviet Union

On the 22nd of June 1941 German forces attacked the largest country in Europe, the Soviet Union. Hitler's plan called for only eight weeks of fighting. Nobody imagined that the war would last for another four years and would completely change the map of Europe. The ground force strength consisted of 1,400 Pz.Kpfw. IIIs and IVs, 770 Pz.Kpfw. 35(t)s and 38(t)s, 250 assault guns and 1,150 Pz.Kpfw. Is and IIs, the latter being obsolete. These vehicles totalled 3,300. The Soviet opponent probably fielded the largest tank fleet in the world, an estimated 22,000 tanks. The vast majority of this force consisted of old and totally obsolete vehicles. On the other hand, the Soviets had the most sophisticated armored vehicles - - the T-34 medium and KV heavy tanks - - in their arsenal. Both would come as a sobering surprise to the Germans since no German tank or antitank gun was able to deal with these MBTs. Nevertheless, the German troops were successful, and an enormous amount of terrain was taken. In many battles, thousands of Soviet tanks were surrounded and destroyed or captured, and hundreds of thousands of soldiers were captured. By the end of the year, German advanced detachments had reached the outskirts of Moscow.

In November the assault was halted. The early winter of 1941 brought temparatures of -20° C (-20° F) as early as mid-November. "General Winter" was an old ally of Russia; Napoleon himself had been stopped and repulsed by this mighty adversary. When on the 5th of December the Soviet counter-offensive was launched, the temperatures fell to -40 to -50° C (-40 to -60° F). German weapons were paralyzed and most of the tanks no longer functioned. The individual German soldiers were ill prepared for a winter campaign, and many died because of the cold.

A careful analysis of the situation on the Eastern Front revealed disturbing truths:

1. The German Panzerwaffe was outclassed by modern Soviet developments. Neither the armor protection nor the weaponry of German tanks was sufficient. Even if the Pz.Kpfw. III and IV could be improved to a certain extent by adding extra armor or by upgunning, these vehicles had to be regarded as being obsolete. The appearance of the Russian T-34 and KV tanks led to a redesign of German tank development, which resulted in the production of Panther and Tiger tanks in 1943.

2. The decision to use Otto cycle engines (mainly produced by Maybach) resulted in comparatively high fuel consumption, which burdened the supply lines. Also, both the starting capability at low temperatures and the degree of efficiency were inferior compared to the Soviet diesel engines. However, since the Maybach engines were generally regarded as being satisfactory, a redesign was not demanded.

It is amazing, however, that despite these severe problems the performance of the German tank formations was so impressive. The reasons for this were many:

1. The organization of the armored formation was tailored for mobile warfare, as was shown in previous campaigns. Shortcomings could be overcome immediately.

2. The widespread supply of wireless radios resulted in a high degree of communication during the battle. Leadership was direct and efficient.

3. Co-operation with other branches of service was exemplary. In particular, the air force had very close links to the ground forces.

4. Crews and engineers were trained at a high level. They were used to the technology and were able to master most problems.

━ ･ ━ ･ ━ ･ ━ ･ ━ ･ ━

The second volume will cover the Panzerwaffe from 1942 until the bitter end. All photos were taken from various Polish archives - Military Institute of History, Central Military Archives, Military Photo Agency, and private sources. Special thanks to Mrs. Kudla for help and cooperation, and Mr. Tomasz Kopanski for support.

Before the War

Lacking their own armored vehicle development during WWI, the Germans pressed a large number of captured British tanks into service. Around this core was formed the force that would become the Panzertruppe. This Mk IV tank, which displays a large Iron Cross next to what remains of the British markings, is being inspected by suitably impressed German officers.

This unique post card shows what appears to be one-fifth of the total German tank production of 1918. With only 20 units produced, the A7V played no important part in the fighting during WWI. The basic design had many shortcomings, the most important being weak cross-country maneuverability.

Towards the end of the war, the A7V was redesigned. The result, an example of which is seen here, was called the A7V-U. As is apparent, it showed many similarities to the contemporary British tanks. The rhomboid shape is very evident in this photo. This — unsuccessful — design did not enter into production.

In 1918 a light tank was developed — the LK II. Due to the restrictions imposed on Germany by the Treaty of Versailles, all files and manufacturing machinery were exported to Sweden. There a limited number of "Strijdsvagn M 21" vehicles were produced, which were used well into the 1930s. Note the early camouflage pattern.

The production of the massive "K-Wagen", an extraordinary heavy tank weighing 150 tons, was finished by the end of WWI. However, both prototypes had to be scrapped. This photo shows the production line at Wegmann in Kassel.

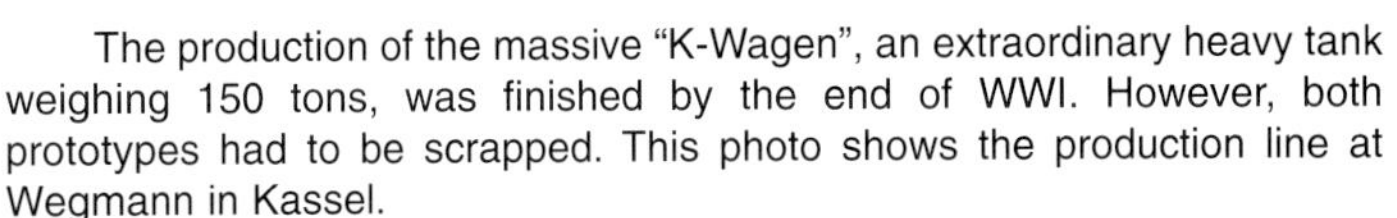

The *Leichtertraktor* was developed during the late 1920s. A small number of these light tanks was produced, which served as experimental vehicles. The armament was a 3.7cm KwK L/45 and a light machine gun. This interesting photo, probably taken during a celebration in 1934/35, shows an improved running gear with greased tracks. Note the black tankers uniform and the *Schutzmütze* (padded beret) that each crew member wears. (F. Schulz)

The *Großtraktor* was another step in the advancement of tank technology. This armored vehicle was developed by several firms, but this photo shows the Rheinmetall version. The main armament consisted of a 7.5cm KwK L/24 gun. The careful evaluation of this vehicle at Kazan, where a variety of spring systems, running gears, transmissions and tracks were tested, brought about valuable results.

This photo depicts the Daimler-Benz version of the *Großtraktor*. It is interesting that long-barreled guns (here a 7.5cm) were in use as early as 1930. It would take another twelve years before such effective guns were introduced to the German tank force. After being transported back to Germany from Kazan, these vehicles served for a short time in the 1.Panzer-Division. Then, however, they ended their service life as monuments, such as this one that has been placed in front of a Panzer regiment headquarters.

When available in sufficient numbers, the Pz.Kpfw. I replaced the dummy tanks. This light tank was a sound design — as a training tank. Cheap and simple, the Pz.Kpfw. I showed all the characteristics of later tanks such as the Tiger. Provided with a rear engine, rotating turret and a radio, the Pz.Kpfw. I was the core of the later-to-be-formed Panzerwaffe, which took their first ride in these vehicles. No serious official or officer would have believed that the Wehrmacht would use the Pz.Kpfw. I in combat. This vehicle (an Ausf. A), photographed while smashing down a small brick wall, is being used in one of the many propaganda shows that were presented from 1934 to 1936.

German infantry troopers help us to gauge the size of a Pz.Kpfw. I Ausf. A as they take a close look at the tank during maneuvers. Apart from their practical uses, these light tanks helped to get the army used to modern technology. This Ausf. A shows all hatches open, which offers an interesting view into the engine compartment. The tactical marking on the turret is a non-standard one. Markings like this differed widely in the mid-30s.

Here Pz.Kpfw.Is of 1.Panzer-Division parade in impressive fashion at a propaganda show at Nuremberg in 1934. Given the inspiring appearance of this fledgling armored force, it is not hard to understand how the roaring engines and rattling tracks would have impressed the average German as well as any foreign observers.

The *Reichstagsgelände* stadium in Nuremberg was the site of many speeches and propaganda extravaganzas. Here Pz.Kpfw. I tanks take part in a combined mock attack of armor and infantry. The Wehrmacht was widely used in this propagandistic manner to boost the morale of the German citizens.

Several 8.8cm Flak 18 guns form a magnificent gun position during a propaganda show in the Marzfeld arena at Nuremberg. As is evident by the number of empty cartridges littering the ground, these guns fired exercise rounds during such shows. Later in the war several German armored vehicles would be armed with this versatile and intimidating weapon.

A line of Pz.Kpfw. I Ausf. As are positioned for display during the *Reichsbauerntag*, a farmers celebration, in 1935. Tank regiments were sent to rural areas as well as to the larger cities. These tanks wear the camouflage of brown or green (maybe both) over gray, which was commonly applied during that period.

Proud tankers pass in review in their Pz.Kpfw. I light tanks. The vehicles are each armed with a pair of 7.92mm MG13 machine guns. Postcards with images like this bearing the title *Unser Heer* - Our Army - were published in large numbers in pre-World War Two Germany.

A number of Pz.Kpfw. Is were issued to the troops without turrets to serve as tank driving school vehicles. This particular vehicle (belonging to the 8th company) is painted in a three-tone camouflage of dark gray, dark green and chocolate brown.

These Pz.Kpfw. Is display different tactical markings than shown in other photos. The rhomboid (note how it compares with the shape of British WWI tanks) was the basic marking for tanks in the German Army. The number "8" at the bottom right corner denotes the company.

Another *Fahrschulwagen* driver training vehicle belonging to a different unit. This one, which is finished in plain dark gray, is fitted with a radio for training purposes. At the beginning of WWII the Germans had a highly trained tank force thanks to the availability of these light tanks.

Pz.Kpfw. I Ausf. A tanks of Panzer-Regiment 5, II.Abteilung, 5.Kompanie parade through the *Brandenburger Tor* (Brandenburg Gate) in Berlin. The tanks show the typical two-tone camouflage of dark gray and chocolate brown. At this early period, the tanks were not yet decorated with any type of cross, the familiar national marking of Germany.

Pz.Kpfw Is also belonging to Pz.Rgt. 5, II.Abteilung, 5.Kompanie are seen here passing in review on *Unter den Linden* avenue. Propaganda parades like this that showcased Germany's growing military might were organized all over Germany, helping to create the hotbed of emotion that existed prior to the coming war.

Crowds of admiring German citizens crowd behind a row of Pz.Kpfw. Is along the side of a street somewhere in Germany to salute their Führer, Adolf Hitler, as he inspects his young tank force. The presence of the national eagle insignia seen on the tank crewmen's berets and jackets indicate that this photo was taken sometime after May 1936.

Two heavy half-tracked prime mover tractors (12-ton *Zugmaschine*, DBs 7, Sd.Kfz. 8) haul troops and tow guns (s.10cm Kanone 18) during a parade. These halftracks offered outstanding cross-country maneuverability combined with high road travel speed and were an integral part of the Panzer division.

A 3.7cm Pak 36 gun is seen in position during a winter maneuver. The gun crew rather successfully uses a white sheet to conceal the shape of the gun. Apparently the soldiers don´t take their job too seriously, as is evident by the bored appearance of the truck drivers. Nevertheless, the antitank gun battalion was yet another important element of a Panzer division.

Hundreds of motorsport events took place during the 1930s. These endurance rallies helped to improve motorcycles and other military vehicles — and created a feeling of fellowship among the participants. In this unique and amusing scene, an elephant borrowed from a circus is employed to recover a Krupp-Protze light truck that has been bogged down in a brook.

In 1938, Austria was incorporated into the German Reich. The amalgamation of the two German-speaking neighboring countries was an important step in the prelude to war. This photo shows an antitank unit entering a town somewhere in Austria. The Krupp-Protze wheeled vehicle shows the specialized body intended for use with the 3.7cm Pak gun.

The occupation of Czechoslovakia helped to replenish the German war arsenal significantly. The LT Vz 38, better known under the German designation Pz.Kpfw. 38(t), helped to establish one division. This photo shows the original Czech version of this tank in its three-tone camouflage and fitted with a combat aerial.

Photographed shortly before the Polish campaign, these early Pz.Kpfw. I Ausf. B *kleine Panzerbefehlswagen* (small armored command vehicles) still lack their machine guns. The aperture for the gun, which is located just below the small cupola, is sealed by a steel plate. Command vehicles were available in large numbers and played an important part during the advance of the German tank force during the Blitzkrieg.

Photographed during the first day of the invasion of Poland, this Panzerbefehlswagen I Ausf. B crosses a wooden bridge. Pioneers have erected eight assault bridges to make access to the bridge easier. A noteworthy change in the basic appearance of the tanks at this time is the addition of the white cross national insignia.

During the Polish campaign the German tanks carried prominent white Greek crosses painted on their hull or turret. These proved to be perfect aiming points for enemy gunners, however. After the first losses, the Germans learned to smear dirt or paint over the crosses to subdue them. The inner parts of the white cross on this particular Pz.Kpfw. I have been painted yellow.

Another column of Pz.Kpfw. I tanks moves into a Polish town. Designed for training purposes, these light tanks were hopelessly obsolete at the time of the Polish campaign, yet they remained in service through most of 1941. No national markings are visible on the lead tank.

The crew of this Pz.Kpfw. II engage in the necessary chore of cleaning the weaponry of their tank — a 20mm cannon and a co-axial 7.29mm machine gun.. Maintenance work like this had to be done in the field and under all conditions. This early Pz.Kpfw. II, with its distinctive rounded bow, displays a large white cross on its turret. Barely visible under the cross is the rhomboid plate with the vehicle number "612".

A Pz.Kpfw. IIb fording a waterhole shows the problems the early tanks had to deal with. Insufficient engine power, unserviceable running gear, and lack of deep-wading capability made such fording attempts during combat most dangerous. The number "II 06" painted on the superstructure indicates that this vehicle is from the 2nd battalion's staff section. A solid white cross is clearly visible on the turret.

Besides the Pz.Kpfw. 38(t), the only tank suitable for tank vs. tank engagements during the Polish campaign was the Pz.Kpfw. III with its 3.7cm gun. Basically a very good design, the early Pz.Kpfw. III suffered from this ineffective armament and weak 30mm-thick armor. This photo was taken after the Western campaign, as evident by the divisional marking of 6.Panzer-Division. Note that the position of the Notek light has been changed.

Used in the fourth and eighth companies, the Pz.Kpfw. IV tanks served as attack support vehicles. Armed with a 7.5cm L/24 gun, they would survey the battlefield and fight against enemy gun positions and heavy tanks. Except for the driver, the entire crew of this Ausf. B is visible at their hatches.

The strange vehicle shown here negotiating a muddy road is a former Austrian ADGZ heavy armored car. These eight-wheelers were used by police units in the Gdansk/Gdynia area. Again the white cross is evident in this obscure photo.

The profile of the ADGZ armored car is shown in this photo. The side hatches are open, illustrating that armor protection was on the lower part of the vehicle. These vehicles were never popular with the German troops. After the first combat in Poland, they were used in an antipartisan role in the Balkans.

Another Panzerbefehlswagen I Ausf. B moves up. The small size of these vehicles is evident by comparing them with the accompanying transport trucks. The interior of the observation and command vehicle was very cramped since the extensive radio equipment took up a great deal of space.

The crew of an Sd.Kfz. 231 armored car evaluates the progress of the German advance. The high degree of communication among German forces during the Polish campaign was one of the reasons for its success. Also, the eight-wheeled recconnaissance vehicles proved to be both versatile and efficient.

The oppression of Polish residents began shortly after the invasion. This photo shows a Jewish religious leader being forced to clean a kleiner Panzerbefehlswagen I Ausf. B. It is noteworthy that Wehrmacht soldiers rather than SS troops or special combat forces seem to have put him in this degrading position.

This impressive shot shows an unarmored Sd.Kfz. 10/4 combat vehicle negotiating a slope. The 1-ton halftrack was a most versatile vehicle. The version here, which is armed with the 2cm Flak 38 gun, quickly became famous as the *Sturmflak* - - the antiaircraft assault vehicle.

A crew member of this kleiner Panzerbefehlswagen I Ausf. B points to the impact of a machine gun bullet visible on the vehicle's cupola. As humorous as the scene might appear, the photo makes clear that the armor of the light German tanks was very thin; an antitank rifle would surely have ended the service life of this kl.Pz.Bef.Wg. I.

A command tank passes a destroyed Polish horse-drawn supply wagon and the team of horses that were killed while providing useful service. Neither Poland nor the German aggressor could do without these old-fashioned transport devices. Again the prominent white cross is evident on the hull.

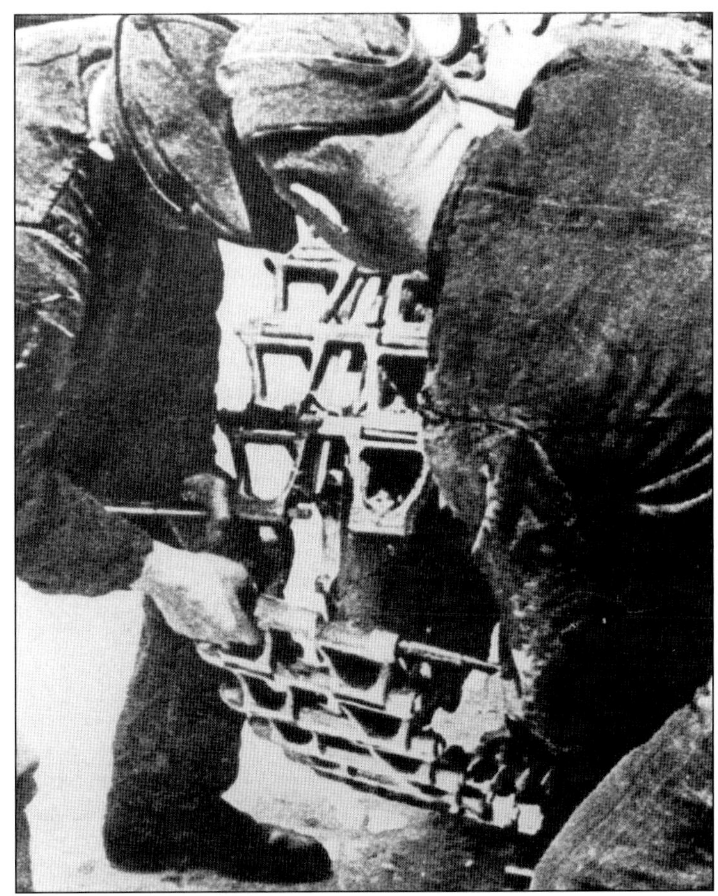

Maintenance was essential and had to be performed at any time and under any conditions. Here two tankers repair a damaged track, an easy job to accomplish with the light Pz.Kpfw. I. This view provides a good close-up look at how the track is assembled.

A barn serves as a shelter and an ersatz garage while two mechanics provide this Pz.Kpfw. I Ausf. A with a thorough maintenance check. The running gear of both the Pz.Kpfw. I and II proved to be prone to mechanical breakdowns.

This Sd.Kfz. 232 *Sechsrad* (six-wheeler) was destroyed by a number of antitank rifle rounds. These old vehicles were phased out after the Polish campaign with only a few surviving in staff sections. Their cross-country performance and armor protection were never sufficient. Of interest is the German cross, whose inner portion has been neatly painted gray to discourage enemy gunners from using it to target the tank.

The Poles employed many specialized railway transport cars. Here one carries an obsolete ex-French FT-17, which is being inspected by a group of camera-conscious German troops. Barely visible in the background is a TKS tankette.

Quite a few old-fashioned FT-17 light infantry tanks were still in service in Poland in 1940. Here some German tankers amuse themselves while examining a captured vehicle in the Brzesc area. No doubt the tank appears to be an antique to the young warriors.

Unternehmung Weserübung - The Occupation of Northern Europe

An infantry squad (mounted on bicycles) takes cover behind a Pz.Kpfw. I during action in Norway in 1940. Although understandable, this was a dangerous practice since any tank would attract enemy fire. Also, the tank could endanger prone soldiers if it should start to drive backwards. This particular vehicle is an Ausf. A of a late production batch, as is evident by the air intake covers of the cooling system.

Another Pz.Kpfw. I Ausf. A of the Panzer-Abteilung z.b.V.40 — the only German tank unit involved in the fighting — prepares to ford a stream. The officer supervises the operation with a look of concern as to whether the tiny tank will be able to do the job.

All three *Neubaufahrzeuge* (NbFz) armored vehicles that were produced were attached to Panzer-Abteilung z.b.V.40 and saw action in the Oslo area of Norway. One vehicle was destroyed, and the two survivors were shipped back to Germany at the end of 1940. The NbFzs were produced in the typical 1930-style design that featured one main and two auxiliary MG turrets. Though impressive, they had no combat value. The complicated running gear is visible in the foreground.

Soldiers climb onto a NbFz to satisfy their curiosity about the vehicle. These "heavy" tanks attracted attention wherever they appeared. It should not be forgotten that though it was obsolete, the NbFz was still an important step in the development of the German tank force.

1940 - The War in the West

The railway system had proven to be the most important means of transportation for all modern armies from the time of the First World War. The Opel Blitz 3-ton trucks shown here are being prepared for shipment to the western border in early 1940. The wooden body on the first truck was non-standard.

A Sd.Kfz. 7 (8-ton halftrack) moves through a Luxembourg town towing the deadly 8.8cm Flak 18 gun. In anticipation of the appearance of heavy French tanks, the crews of the AA guns were given crash courses in antitank gunnery. Though the "88" was most effective in this role, its crews had a dangerous life behind their guns. Note that the license plate of the artillery tractor was obscured by the censors.

Approaching a destroyed bridge, a Pz.Kpfw. II Ausf. C silences enemy positions. Pioneers have already successfully crossed this Belgian river, as is evident by the rafts visible on the far side. A Nazi flag has been placed atop the tank's hull for easy identification from the air.

A Pz.Kpfw. III Ausf. E crosses over a pontoon bridge that pioneers have erected over a stream. The simple act of the tank crossing the bridge was a demonstration of Germany's ability to resolve any problems that might arise during modern mobile warfare.

This Pz.Kpfw. IV Ausf. D crosses a bridge in the Low Countries in 1940. The tank wears the narrow white German crosses that were commonly seen during the Western campaign. It is also equipped with five smoke candle dischargers, which was typical for German tanks and StuGs in that year.

A StuG III Ausf. A passes by a tank obstacle as it crosses the border into France on May 10, 1940. The assault artillery was a new service that saw its first action in the invasion of France. Intended for infantry support, the StuGs proved to be most effective. Still lacking the Sd.Kfz. 253 observer´s vehicles, standard Sd.Kfz. 251 halftracks had to be used, as exemplified by the vehicle following the StuG.

It was originally planned that the StuG battalions would receive specialized armored halftracks (Sd.Kfz. 252s) to carry out ammunition resupply duties in forward areas. Since these vehicles could not be delivered in time, a number of Pz.Kpfw. I Ausf. As were converted for this purpose. Here one of these supply tanks travels through a destroyed town.

A number of armored pioneer companies were provided with Pz.Kpfw. I Ausf. Bs that had been converted to carry demolition charges. The devices fitted to the rear deck of the charge-laying tank allowed a charge to be placed in a designated area to clear a path for the troops. The tactical use of these *kleine Ladungsleger* was rather limited, so it is not likely that they were often used.

The Czech Pz.Kpfw. 38(t) played an important part in Germany´s highly mobile warfare. Rommel preferred these fast and reliable vehicles for his raids, which dramatically illustrated the penetration abilities of armored formations. Here an Ausf. B races down a roadway.

A Pz.Kpfw. III Ausf. E tows a disabled *Einheitsdiesel* truck. This medium tank was intended for tank vs. tank fighting. However, neither armament (3.7cm) nor armor protection (30mm maximum) proved to be sufficient for this task. It is interesting that the powerful 5cm KwK 40 gun was available in 1940 since the ordnance bureau´s policy supposedly prevented the use of the gun before 1941.

This well-known propaganda photo shows a Pz.Kpfw. IV Ausf. B or C of Pz.Rgt. 7, 10.Panzer-Division, as is indicated by the silhouette of the charging Bison stencilled on the lower left of the turret. The short-barreled 7.5cm gun is shown to advantage here. Also of interest is the antenna deflector attached to the gun.

A Sd.Kfz. 223, followed by a Sd.Kfz. 222, passes through a French city. These armored cars were fitted with a large frame antenna, as most command and liaison vehicles were until 1942. Though effective, the conspicuous antenna attracted enemy attention, resulting in relatively high losses. Note the small number "5" next to the registration plate.

Parked in front of the Gothic cathedral in Rheims, this Pz.Kpfw. II shows typical markings of the Western campaign. Barely visible under the turret number is the rhomboid tactical symbol of a tank unit. Interestingly enough, the rear mudguards of this Ausf. C or A are modified, lacking the large flaps.

The war against France was even a greater success for Germany than the victory over Poland. This Pz.Kpfw. II is being used to transport some of the thousands of French prisoners that were taken. Generally, the French prisoners were treated well, but this practice changed significantly in Russia, where thousands died of starvation. Again the tactical marking was retouched by the censors; note the black marks on the right rear of the hull.

This Pz.Kpfw. II is from a later production lot. In 1940, production of Ausf. C started, featuring add-on armor on the turret´s and hull´s front plates. The original rounded bow was reinforced by a box-like structure. Older versions were subsequently reworked during repair depot maintenance. This photo was probably taken during one of the many small victory reviews in France during the summer of 1940.

A column of early Sd.Kfz. 251/1 (Ausf. B) halftracks roll down a tree-lined road. These versatile vehicles were available only in limited numbers during the invasion of France. The units equipped with these armored personnel carriers (here 1.Panzer-Division) suffered significantly lower losses than other infantry units. The leading Hanomag is carrying on its right mudguard the emblem of the division (white oakleaf) and the markings of 10th company of the motorized infantry battalion.

The armor of the light tanks was anything but sufficient. An artillery hit tore apart the entire side of the turret of this Pz.Kpfw. II. It belonged to 20.Panzer-Division, as the faint symbol of the Brandenburg Gate indicates.

Many Pz.Kpfw. Is were converted to ammunition and supply carriers by removing the turret. While this *Munitionsschlepper* I (ammunition carrier) passes through a devastated French town, its crew members take a fascinated look at some typical debris of war.

This overloaded Krupp-Protze light wheeled vehicle is transporting POWs, among them some colonial soldiers, to a camp. Although very useful and reliable, these vehicles suffered from limited cross-country abilities since they lacked a driven front axle.

"Bourrasque", a French Char B1 bis tank, receives inspection by German soldiers. Many French tanks were found deserted due to minor mechanical problems. In most fighting, the French tanks were split up, a tactic that was no match for the German tactic of concentrated breakthrough. Wherever an organized defense could be established, however, the German assault came to a halt. Judged by their armor and armament, tanks like these heavy tanks were superior to any German vehicle.

The French tanks, heavily armored and armed, were dangerous enemies to the German tank troops. Here a Renault R-35 lays abandoned in a field. It is painted in the typical French camouflage scheme of sand, brown and green stripes outlined with black lines. The R-35's company insignia is visible on the turret.

This French Char B1 bis was totally destroyed by an internal explosion. Both guns are visible, the 47mm in the turret and the 75mm in the bow. The Germans had no tank comparable to this one, but sophisticated tactics and effective communication during the battle more than compensated for this shortcoming.

Shortly after the invasion of France, the Germans prepared for the planned invasion of Great Britain. This photo shows a prototype of the *Schwimmpanzer* II, a Pz.Kpfw. II Ausf. C that is carried through the water by a large pontoon. Equipment like this was later used along with deep-wading tanks during Operation "Barbarossa".

Pz.Kpfw. I Ausf. A, Pz.Rgt. 1, Reichsbauerntag, 1935

In the early years of Hitler's rule, tanks were widely used to impress both the German population and foreign countries. This Pz.Kpfw. I Ausf. A was displayed with units of Pz.Rgt. 1 at the German farmer's convention in Bückeburg in 1935. The vehicle was finished in gray with broad chocolate-brown stripes, a common camouflage in this period. Markings consisted of a white triangle with a red dot in the middle (1.Kompanie) positioned at the rear of the turret. The Wehrmacht had no common system for tactical markings in those early days, so many units tested their own ideas. Most of them were short-lived.

Pz.Kpfw. IV Ausf. A, 3.Panzer-Division, northern Poland, early September 1939

The Pz.Kpfw. IV Ausf. A was designed to monitor the combat of the main battle tanks (Pz.Kpfw. II and III). The fourth company of the tank regiments was provided with this vehicle. With its short-barreled 7.5cm gun, it could engage and destroy antitank positions and heavy enemy tanks. However, the armor protection (14.5mm with the Ausf. A) proved to be inadequate. At this time no German tank showed any camouflage scheme; all armored vehicles were painted in plain dark gray. This particular Ausf. A shows the full range of tactical markings introduced prior to the Polish campaign -- large white German crosses and vehicle numbers over-painted with mud or yellow paint. The tank carries facines on the engine deck, which were often used to negotiate swampy terrain.

Pz.Kpfw. 38(t) Ausf. A, Pz.Abt. 67, 3.leichte-Division, southern Poland, September 1939

The fast and reliable Pz.Kpfw. 38(t) was used in the light divisions, the so-called schnelle Truppen, or rapid forces. This concept was not successful, however, and was soon rejected. This Pz.Kpfw. 38(t) Ausf. A of 3.leichte-Division, which is still equipped with a Czech combat antenna, has standard white German crosses painted on its turret. The vehicle numbers were painted on small rhomboid plates that were attached to both sides and the rear of the hull, another very common practice during the early campaigns. The prominent white crosses proved to be excellent aiming points for enemy gunners, thus many units covered them with mud or toned down the center with yellow paint.

Pz.Kpfw. II Ausf. c, Pz.Rgt. 36, 4.Panzer-Division, Warsaw, September 1939

This Pz.Kpfw. II Ausf. c of the staff platoon of Pz.Rgt. 36, 4.Panzer-Division is painted in the standard dark gray paint scheme of 1939. The vehicle number and the German cross have been defaced to avoid recognition by the enemy. Vehicles like this were used mainly for liasion and reconnaissance duties. The bulk of the tank force of 4.Panzer-Division consisted of Pz.Kpfw. Is and Pz.Kpfw. IIs during the Polish campaign.

Pz.Kpfw. II Ausf. b, Pz.Rgt. 7, 10.Panzer-Division, France, May 1940

This Pz.Kpfw. II displays the official insignia of Pz.Rgt. 7, a charging bison, stencilled on the turret sides. No national marking is visible. The vehicle number, "542", is carried on a small rhomboid plate, and the company number, "5", is repeated on the turret. 10.Panzer-Division was attached to XIX.Panzer Korps under Guderian's command during the French campaign.

kl. Panzerbefehlswagen I Ausf. B, 4.Panzer-Division, France, May 1940

As early as 1940 the first command tanks based on the Pz.Kpfw. I were phased out. This particular kl. Panzerbefehlswagen I Ausf. B was converted to an ambulance and used by the leader of the medical section, giving him some armor protection. A large red cross was painted over the German cross. Additionally, a Red Cross flag was added to the antenna.

StuG III Ausf. A, Sturmartillerie Batterie 640, Regiment "Großdeutschland", France, May 1940

Two batteries of assault guns took part in the invasion of France. Designed to lead the infantry assault, the Sturmgeschütz proved to be a very successful weapon. Equipped with the same 7.5cm gun as the Pz.Kpfw. IV Ausf. A through F1, these vehicles could take on gun positions and enemy tanks. Typical of the Ausf. A were the large stowage boxes fitted to the track covers. The StuGs of the battery attached to "Großdeutschland" carried German crosses (Balkenkreuze) on the sides of the superstructure and on the top. The vehicle number was reduced to a two-digit system (platoon number and vehicle number). Other units used letters and numbers.

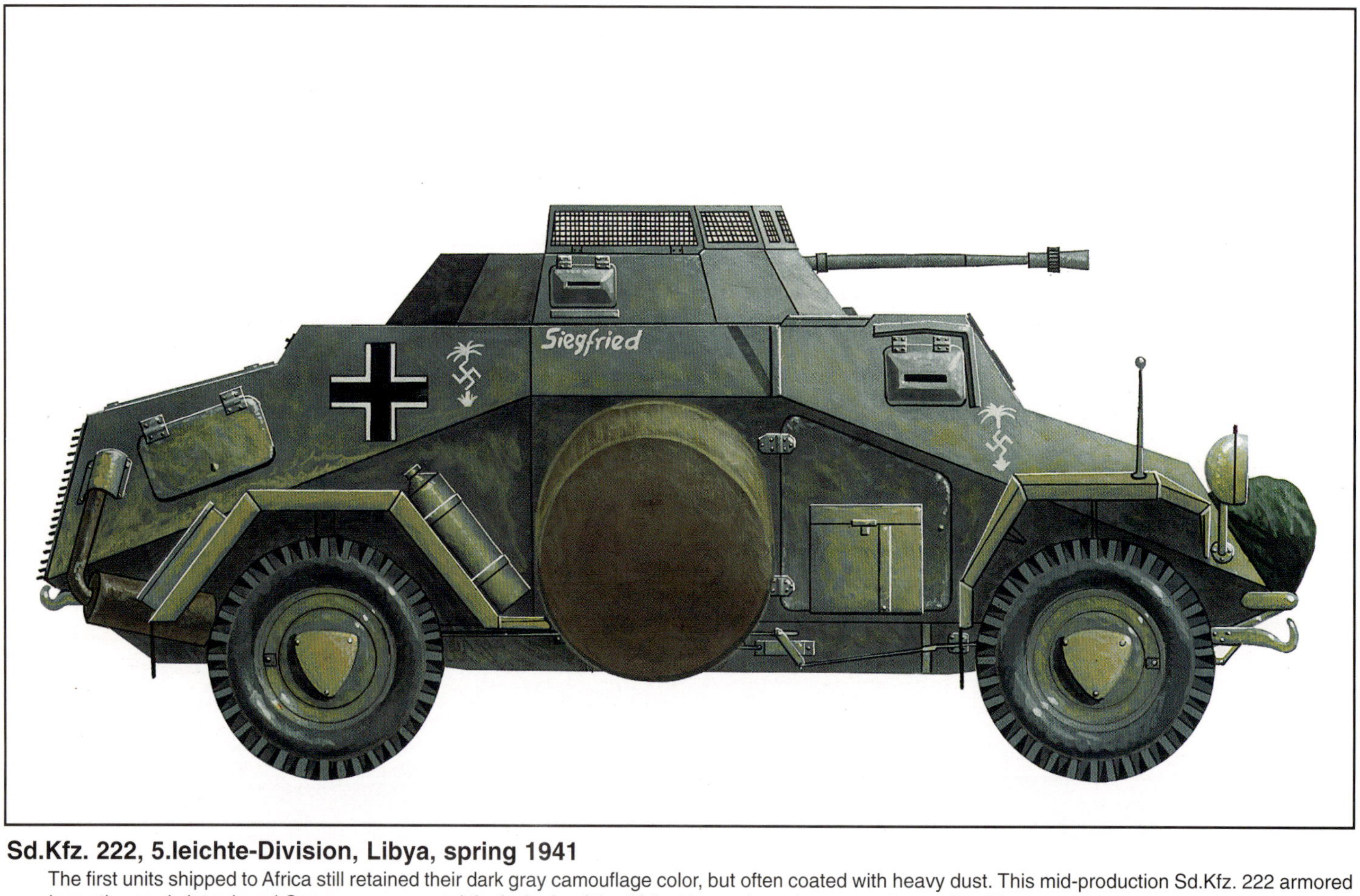

Sd.Kfz. 222, 5.leichte-Division, Libya, spring 1941

The first units shipped to Africa still retained their dark gray camouflage color, but often coated with heavy dust. This mid-production Sd.Kfz. 222 armored car shows the newly introduced German crosses and the insignia of the Afrika Korps, the palm tree and swastika. The personal name "Siegfried" was added by the crew, as was occasionally the case with German vehicles.

Pz.Kpfw. III Ausf. G, 2.Panzer-Division, Greece, April 1941

In late 1940 many Pz.Kpfw. IIIs were retrofitted with the 5.cm KwK L/42, and the later production batches of the Ausf. G left the factory with this more powerful gun. Frontal armor was reinforced to 50mm, making the Pz.Kpfw. III a well-balanced tank. This Ausf. G is decorated with a full array of markings. The German crosses were of the later style, black with white outlines, which was used until the end of the war. The tactical marking of 2.Panzer-Division was painted on the hull beside the chassis number. The white vehicle number was not applied to the turret, but appeared on the hull, as well. The most prominent location, the side of the turret, was occupied by the regimental badge.

Pz.Kpfw. III Ausf. F, Pz.Rgt. 31, 5.Panzer-Division, France, June 1941

The Pz.Kpfw. III was the mainstay of Germany's tank formations from 1939 to 1942. Designed for tank vs. tank engagements, the first versions were equipped with the 3.7cm KwK, although development of the more powerful 5cm gun was soon finished. In 1940 the gun proved to be useless against the heavily armored French tanks. This Ausf. F wears the new-style German crosses outlined in white, the result of one of the lessons learned in the Polish campaign. The vehicle number is painted on the hull rather than on the turret. The number "542" denotes the position of the tank in the division: 5th company, 4th platoon, 2nd vehicle.

Panzerbefehlswagen 35(t), Pz.Abt. 65, 6.Panzer-Division, Russia, June 1941

During the initial stage of Operation "Barbarossa", a number of divisions were equipped with the former Czech Pz.Kpfw. 35(t) light tank. Not as popular as the Pz.Kpfw. 38(t), these vehicles suffered problems with their air pressure brake system, especially during the harsh Russian winter when they tended to freeze. This particular tank is a command tank, as is evident by the frame antenna behind the fixed turret. Again, the tactical numbers are painted on rhomboid plates (A03 = 1st Bn., 3rd vehicle). The meaning of the badge on the turret in unknown.

Pz.Kpfw. I Ausf. B, 7.Panzer-Division, Russia, August 1941

Immediately before the invasion of the Soviet Union, the tactical markings used on German tanks were modified and standardized. This Pz.Kpfw. I is a good example. The German cross now featured a black center to make it less conspicious. Large turret numbers were introduced with many units, either red or black with white outlines. The tactical marking of 7.Panzer-Division is still painted in yellow.

Panzerbefehlswagen III Ausf. H, 15.Panzer-Division, North Africa, winter 1941
This command tank still shows the dark gray base color. The desert sand, however, concealed this dark shade rather quickly. The Panzerbefehlswagen III has its German cross national marking painted on the turret. The tactical number "III" denotes the third battalion. As was often the case with armored vehicles in North Africa, this tank carries a lot of extra equipment.

Pz.Kpfw. III Ausf. J, Pz.Rgt. 11, 6.Panzer-Division, Russia, winter 1941/42
This vehicle received a scruffy camouflage scheme of white blotches. No markings are visible except the vehicle number. Note that the tank, which belongs to the 10th company, carries an air recognition Nazi flag over the engine deck. The 5cm KwK L/42 gun equipped Ausf. J were sent to Russia in late 1941 as reinforcements to replace the losses during the initial phase of Operation "Barbarossa"..

Pz.Kpfw. IV Ausf. E, II.Abteilung, Pz.Rgt. 8, 15.Panzer-Division, Libya, 1941/42

The organizational structure of 1939 still being valid, the "heavy" Pz.Kpfw. IV tanks were still issued to the fourth and eighth companies of the tank divisions. Although the combat principles were unchanged as well, the tactical use of tanks in the desert was much different. With the duty of monitoring the battlefield handed over to the artillery, the Pz.Kpfw. IV was now being used in the same way as the Pz.Kpfw. III. However, its gun was not accurate against moving targets, and the armor penetration was weak. The armor protection came to the standard of the Pz.Kpfw. III -- 50mm at the front. This particular Ausf. E shows a dark sand camouflage sprayed over the dark gray base color and large vehicle numbers on the sides of the turret. The division's emblem is painted on a red disc.

StuG III Ausf. E, StuG.Abt. 184, Russia, winter 1941/42

During the first winter in Russia almost anything was used to camouflage frontline vehicles. The vehicle here is wearing a lime whitewash, but notice that the Balkenkreuz and the vehicle's name, still visible on the gray base color, were not whitewashed over. This StuG III Ausf. E carries a lot of extra gear on the engine deck, which was a widespread method of tranporting supplies. Parts of StuG.Abt. 184 practiced a simple but unique marking system that was probably used within only one battery: all assault guns received the name of particular wild cat -- "Leopard" in this case.

The Birth of the Afrika Korps

A Pz.Kpfw. IV Ausf. D is being directed to its position in the sandy North African terrain. This vehicle is still finished in plain dark panzer gray. The sand, however, will soon change this appearance. Note the light color of the paint on the inner side of the open turret hatch. The tank carries a lot of extra equipment and the famous *Rommelkiste* (Rommel box) at the rear of the turret, which was typical for most German tanks. Note the five smoke candle dischargers mounted on the exhaust system, they were very useful in the open North African terrain during tank duels.

This photo displays the grim reality of North Africa — seemingly endless roads stretching to the distant horizon across a vast desert. The great distances covered by the fighting vehicles were wearing on both man and machine. The mixed column consists of Pz.Kpfw. III Ausf. G and H and some armored cars.

Reconnaissance vehicles like this Sd.Kfz. 231 eight-wheeled armored car were in common use during the succcessful German advance of 1941/42. Fast and reliable, the recce units scouted the situation and provided important information to the leadership. This vehicle carries the 1.4m rod antenna in an unusual position at the side of the turret instead of on top of it.

The crew of this 2cm Flak 30 gun surveys the skies while transport vehicles pass behind them on the road. Vigilance and protection against air raids was essential since an air attack in the open terrain of North Africa could inflict disastrous results.

A column of Sd.Kfz. 10 1-ton halftracks belonging to an antitank unit move up to the front line. The original dark gray paint scheme that they wear really stands out in this photo, creating a distinct contrast with the sand-colored terrain.

A Panzerbefehlswagen III Ausf. H leads a tank column through the desert. This command tank was fitted with a dummy gun resembling the 5.cm KwK L/42. The 2m and the 1.4m rod antennae are both clearly visible; the larger frame antenna on the engine deck can just barely be seen.

Waiting for action, the crew of this Pz.Kpfw. III Ausf. G looks rather bored. The 5cm KwK L/42 gun has been fitted with a protective covering to prevent dust from intruding into the recoil mechanism. As was a common practice, a lot of extra equipment is stored on the vehicle. This was essential in the desert. The tank has apparently been camouflaged with the application of irregular yellow stripes over the gray base color. The dust would have further improved the camouflage. Note the tactical markings and the splotchy appearance of the *Kübelwagen* in the foreground.

An 8-ton halftrack serves as an artillery tractor as it moves up to the front with the ultimate tank killer, the 8.8cm Flak 36. Since the British had a large number of heavily armored tanks like the Matilda and the Valentine, these guns were most valuable. The deadly combination of halftracks and "88s" was often employed to resolve dangerous situations during both assaults and defensive operations.

This interesting photo shows an 8.8cm Flak gun in full recoil. Although the practice was forbidden, the gun was sometimes fired from the trailer in an emergency situations. This put excess stress on the carriage and brakes. The gunners wear khaki tropical field caps, headgear that was popular with Afrika Korps vehicle crews.

A tank platoon takes a breather while a large column of trucks rolls by. The tanks show that they have been oversprayed with desert yellow paint, while the wheeled vehicles retain their dark gray color. The vehicle numbers are still visible on the small rhomboid plate of the Pz.Kpfw. II, indicating that the photo was taken in the initial stage of the campaign.

A Sd.Kfz. 251/1 Ausf. C, with a welded body, follows a Pz.Kpfw. III through the open desert. The vehicle is finished in sand yellow and displays a prominent national insignia. The armored halftracks were very versatile, but the German war industry was never able to produce a satisfactory number of these vehicles.

Panzer troops of the Deutsches Afrika Korps (DAK) share some small talk with some fellow soldiers. The Pz.Kpfw. IIs seen here are from a later production lot, Ausf. F or G. Although improved, they were hopelessly obsolete by the time of the Africa campaign and were used mainly in reconnaissance roles. These vehicles probably belonged to the 15.Panzer-Division.

This photo shows one of the most famous vehicles of the DAK. This captured British AEC armored command vehicle, nicknamed "Moritz", served as a mobile command post for Gen. Crüwell´s staff. Three of these AEC ACVs were captured from the British 2nd Armoured Division in April 1941 at Mekili. "Moritz" still retains the original British disruptive paint scheme, but carries German markings. Sitting alongside "Moritz" is a Pz.Kpfw. III Ausf. H.

A Panzerbefehlswagen III Ausf. H command vehicle traverses the desert terrain along with several Italian infantrymen. A German radio set is visible behind the trailer. Note how extra jerry cans and other stowage has been secured at the rear of the hull of the tank.

A Pz.Kpfw. IV Ausf. E of the 15.Panzer-Division follows in the sandy wake of some Pz.Kpfw. IIIs as they all transport foot soldiers of the Afrika Korps across the North African desert. The troops riding atop the tanks are fully equipped, indicating that they probably will see action soon. Note how their helmets are also painted a desert sand color.

Smiling at their good fortune, Afrika Korps panzer troops take some time after a battle to pose for a photograph and point out where a British 2-pounder shell, which is still stuck in the cupola, had struck their tank. This photo was taken near Tobruk in September 1941.

This 8-ton halftrack apparently was deserted by its crew. The vehicle looks as if it has been looted. Note the British helmet hanging on the right headlight and the gas mask decorating the radiator grill. The vehicle´s color seems to be sand yellow. The "WL" prefix on the black and white license plate on the bumper is the service code that indicates that this halftrack was in the service of the Luftwaffe. Note the two registration numbers.

Mechanics perform some maintenance work on an early model 8-ton halftrack. Note that parts of the running gear have been removed. Though the German halftrack prime movers were most successful in their service, they were also complicated pieces of machinery subject to problems, as this photo shows. It is important to remember that none of the armored vehicles of the Panzerwaffe could have operated to its full potential without the assistance of the repair crews.

The commander of 15.Panzer-Division recce company gives new orders. The 2m rod antenna on his Sd. Kfz. 222 has been adorned with a pennant showing a *Totenkopf*, the Death's Head symbol of German tank units. The amount of extra equipment that has been packed onto the armored reconnaissance vehicle is noteworthy. The Zündapp KS 750 motorcycle seen at left was used as a liaison vehicle.

This 8.8cm Flak gun is being used in a more traditional artillery role as it provides support fire during an advance. One gunner can be seen standing at the gun looking at his *Folgezeiger* data transmitting system, while the commander supervises the action. It is noteworthy that the gun has no shield, leaving the crew without protection.

A Krupp-Protze gun tractor for a 3.7cm antitank gun passes by a palm tree somewhere near Tripoli. The gray vehicle is completely covered with dust, creating a most effective camouflage. Until later in the war, when the number of self-propelled guns on tracked chassis increased, artillery tractors like this one were essential for the success of the Panzerwaffe.

The Afrika Korps suffered from limited supplies in almost every respect, so Rommel was compelled to make use of a lot of captured equipment. Seen here, however, is a newly-arrived Pz.Kpfw. III Ausf. H being unloaded from a ship. The tank appears to be sand yellow, while the trucks are dark gray. Note the large identification numbers painted on the turret of the tank.

British soldiers inspect a completely destroyed Pz.Kpfw. I Ausf. A. The wreck is painted sand yellow and shows late-style turret markings consisting of large red numbers trimmed in white. Never intended for combat, the light tanks were hopelessly antiquated by the time the war was underway.

This Pz.Kpfw. I is being loaded onto a flatbed trailer for transportion to a vehicle dump. With the production and arrival in North Africa of heavier and more powerful models of German AFVs, the Pz.Kpfw. I became more and more outclassed. The vehicle looks undamaged and will probably be sent home for evaluation.

The North African desert created its own problems for the Afrika Korps, and the extremely rough terrain in the Balkans constantly reminded the Panzerwaffe troops there that they, too, were in for a difficult campaign. Here a Sd.Kfz. 69 Krupp-Protze maneuvers carefully across a railway line. These wheeled vehicles were designed for use with the 3.cm Pak 36 gun.

Young Yugoslavian peasant girls take a curious look at a Panzerbefehlswagen III Ausf. G command tank and the equally youthful soldiers who ride atop it. The long distances travelled by the German troops in the mountainous terrain of the Balkans could be fraught with many problems, especially logistic support, so each vehicle had to carry dozens of jerry cans and spare parts. The vehicle's dummy gun is clearly visible in this photo.

Here some soldiers take advantage of the natural water source of a stream to clean up their vehicles. The light trucks are Mercedes-Benz type 340, Kfz. 16. The doors have been removed. Note that some of the soldiers are wearing the white uniform intended for camp service.

Elements of 11.Panzer-Division are shown here during the victory parade in Belgrade, Yugoslavia. The vehicles passing in review are command tanks belonging to the staff company. The saluting officer in the center is General von Kleist.

This StuG III Ausf. D belonging to an unidentified Sturmgeshütz-Abteilung apparently lacks its gun. The assault gun is interesting since it displays a square symbol (instead of the typical identification number) and a more elongated white cross on the turret. Tanks were often used to impress the population and to create a noticable presence.

This photo shows General von Kleist (center) as viewed from behind as he observes the victory parade in Belgrade. A Pz.Kpfw. IV Ausf. E passes in front of the commander of 11.Panzer-Division, who is standing next to von Kleist. Barely visible on the superstructure of the tank is a stencilled version of the unofficial division symbol — a ghost (*Gespenster*).

Another view of the victory parade in Belgrade. The passing tank, a Pz.Kpfw. III Ausf. F or G, carries a remarkable amount of extra equipment. Note the smoke candle rack at the right rear. This tank is fortunate to be able to participate in the celebration since a number of the Pz.Kpfw IIIs were lost due to accidents during the Balkan campaign.

Barbarossa - The Invasion of the Soviet Union

Vehicles of an unidentified unit are being loaded onto a rail transport to be shipped to the eastern borders prior to the attack against Russia. The variety of types is noteworthy; the German industry was never able to supply uniform equipment. This fact made proper resupply difficult, which all too often resulted in the loss of vehicles due to minor damage. The motorcycle is a (formerly) French Gnome et Rhone, one of the thousands of vehicles captured during the French campaign.

A tank unit, possibly part of 10.Panzer-Division belonging to Heeresgruppe Mitte, waits for railway shipment to the front. The first three vehicles are Panzerbefehlswagen III Ausf. H command vehicles, possibly belonging to the battalion staff section. These command tanks have been disguised with a fake 5cm KwK L/42 gun.

Traffic jam on the Eastern Front. Situations like this one were quite common since established roads were rare in Russia. At least one soldier, the motorcyclist near the bottom right corner of the photo, uses the delay to take a much-needed rest. Note again the remarkable variety of vehicles.

Here a platoon of light tanks passes by an antitank gun unit. The leading tank is a Pz.Kpfw. II Ausf.C; the following is a Pz.Kpfw. I Ausf. B. The 5cm Pak 38 was the most powerful German antitank gun of this period. Basically a very good gun, it became obsolete with appearance of the T-34 medium and the KV heavy tanks.

A column of Pz.Kpfw. 38(t) tanks on the march. Altogether 625 Pz.Kpfw. 38(t)s and 35 command version were used during the opening phase of Operation "Barbarossa". This photo is interesting since the last vehicle in the column is manned by a cameraman from a propaganda unit. German propaganda was as successful as it was thanks to daring reporters like the one shown here.

The crew members of a Pz.Kpfw. IV emerge from their tank to take a break. The early commander´s cupola is shown to advantage, along with the markings indicating the crew's "kills" — two tanks and a steam ship. Note the mixture of gray and black caps, jackets and trousers worn by the crew.

This interesting shot shows a tank trooper sharing rations with a young boy atop a *Tauchpanzer* IV wading tank, which is identifiable by the perforated frame mounted on the turret´s front plate. The gun and deflector are clearly visible in this photo. With Operation "Sea Lion" abandoned, the bulk of the Tauchpanzers went to 18.Panzer-Division, which crossed the River Bug underwater on 22nd June 1941. For uniform enthusiasts, this close-up shows an early pattern jacket with piped collar and the black *Feldmütze* sidecap, which was being issued by the time of Operation "Barbarossa".

An early StuG III, possibly an Ausf. B, negotiates a river bank after fording a river in the initial stage of Operation "Barbarossa". Orginally intended for infantry support, the assault guns would later find their destiny in defending against the masses of Soviet tanks.

This impressive shot shows another StuG III involved in combat in a corn field. The commander surveys the battlefield using his periscope. His hatches remain open during battle. Note the two-piece gun cleaning kit stored in the rack on side of the hull.

A damaged Pz.Kpfw. IV Ausf. E is being repaired in a forest workshop. Though its drive sprocket is broken, the vehicle was kept in running condition by repositioning the track around the frontal return roller and running wheel. A large crane, possibly mounted on a tank, is removing the engine.

Chasing the enemy, a column of tanks plows through a Russian corn field. The leading tanks are Pz.Kpfw. IIIs, followed by a Pz.Kpfw. I Ausf. B. Since they were only used for recconnaissance purposes, every fight was especially dangerous for the light tanks.

This impressive, and apparently unposed, photo shows a T-34 Model 1940 that has been rammed by a StuG III Ausf. B. The Soviet crew hides in the tank, while German soldiers try to open the turret hatch. The soldiers standing on top of the T-34 are crew members of the StuG. Note their apparent head injuries.

An assault gun unit churns up an already overused route during an advance over the vast plains of central Russia. A column of support trucks is visible in the distance. Apparently there is no danger of encountering enemy forces. One detail of interest is how the StuGs have been fitted with protective tarpaulins.

Taken from the perspective of the German soldiers positioned in the grass in the foreground, this photo shows Soviet POWs filing past advancing German troops toward an uncertain future. Of the hundreds of thousands of prisoners taken, only some 20% survived. The leading armored halftrack is a Sd.Kfz. 253 artillery forward observer´s vehicle.

A cavalry platoon of 1.Kavallerie Division (1st Cavalry Division) passes destroyed Soviet armor, an OT-133 flame thrower based on the T-26 and a T-34. In the background lies the blown-up remains of another T-34. Note that the horses carry forage bags around their necks. The presence of these horses is further evidence of pre-twentieth century military technology that was still in use even as the prowess of armored vehicles was being established.

Two German motorcyclists intently study a map as they discuss their current situation. The motorcycle reconnaissance units were famous, their reports often deciding the course of the fighting. Note the helmet attached to the storage bag hanging at the side of the motorcylce.

This propaganda photo shows a Pz.Kpfw. 35(t) towing a toy armored car. Humorous (or cynical) shots like this were often used to cheer up the German population back home. This one seems to imply that the end of another fast and easy Blitzkrieg is at hand.

A crater is the final resting place for a BT-7 light tank, which was hit by a 250-kg (560-lb) bomb by a dive-bomber. The assistance of the Luftwaffe was an essential element in the success achieved during the early Blitzkrieg years. Here a German column, again composed of a mixture of vehicles, passes the destroyed tank.

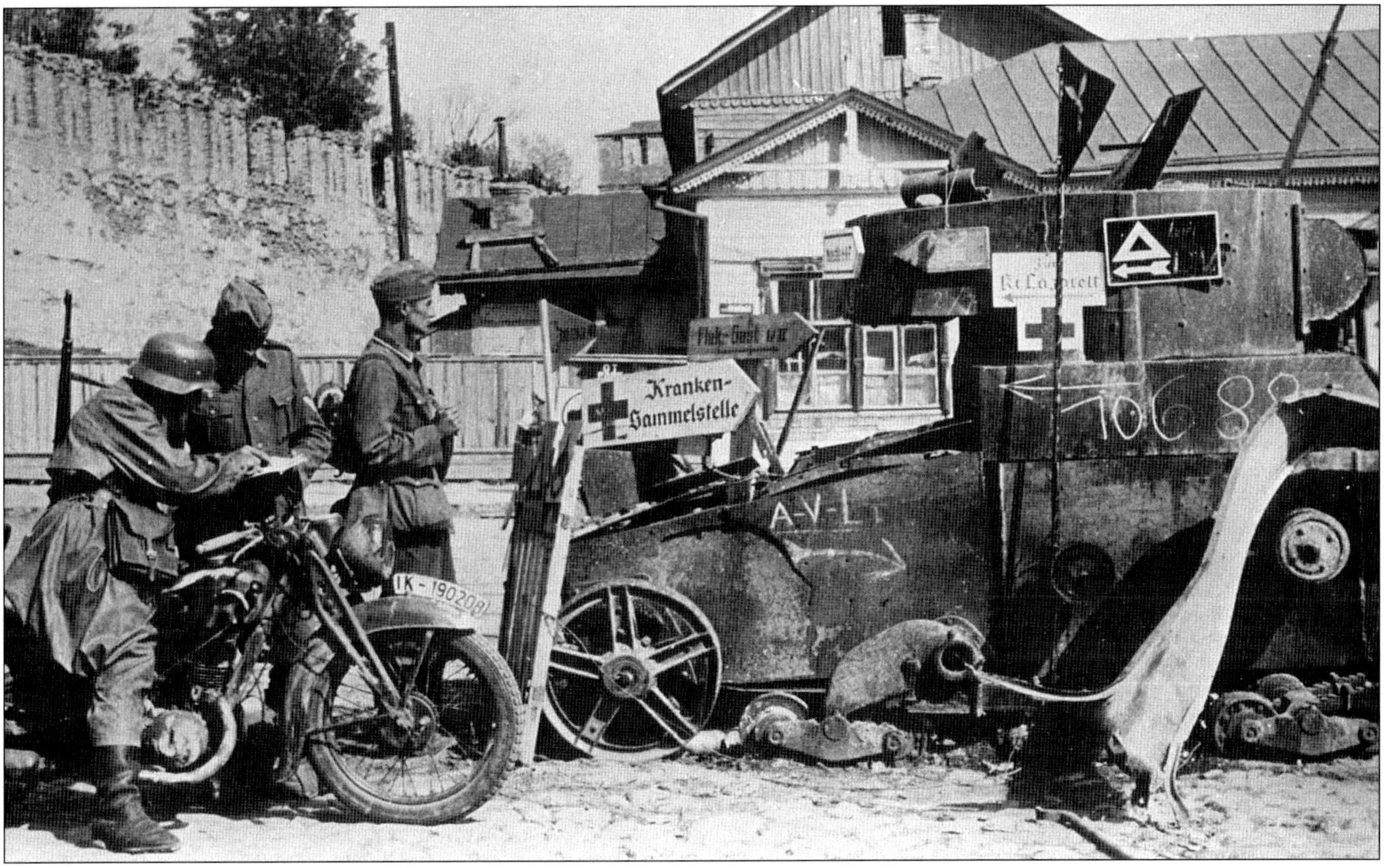

Photographed in the Smolensk area in August 1941, this demolished T-26 Model 37, having been knocked out of the war, now serves ingloriously as a traffic signpost. Note the Luftwaffe unit pennant attached to the tank and the license plate affixed to the motorcycle.

A platoon of Kfz. 69 Krupp-Protze towing 3.7cm Pak 36 guns moves through a Russian village as the townspeople look on. The German troops were often welcomed by the local population, who had bad experiences under Stalin´s suppression. The Germans failed to fulfill their hopes, however, thus paving the way for the rise of partisan groups.

This early Sd.Kfz. 7 8-ton halftrack tows an 8.8cm Flak 18 AA gun to the next battle. Just as in the French campaign, the heavy AA batteries were often the last hope against heavy enemy tanks. Many touch-and-go combat situations were resolved thanks to this versatile and powerful gun.

A crew member lowers down the rear support of an 8.8cm Flak 18. The AA guns used in ground combat were often not camouflaged since they could rely on their long-range antitank capability for protection. Further, sometimes the course of a battle did not allow this luxury.

Dramatic moments during an attack. Photographed from under the gun of a Pz.Kpfw. 38(t), a Soviet tank blows up. Although the 38(t)s were better than the German light tanks, the days of successful use of the former Czech tanks were gone now that they were facing superior Soviet armor.

This similar photo shows a Pz.Kpfw. III Ausf. H passing a burning Soviet support vehicle. The short-barreled 5cm gun on this tank was much more powerful than the earlier 3.7cm gun. Though it was effective in the desert war, it could not deal a death blow to a T-34 or KV heavy tank.

Sturmflak at the front! Flak gun troops put their gun to deadly use during a street fight. These guns were quite effective throughout the war; almost any resistance could be swept away by the repeated blasts of the 2cm or 3.7cm Flak gun.

The 3.7cm Pak 35/36 was a good gun — by 1934 standards. However, by the time of the campaign in the West, it had already shown that its armor penetration was too weak. Hopelessly outclassed and ineffective in the East, the 3.7cm gun was nicknamed *Heeresanklopfgerät* — door knocker— by the German troops.

A thoroughly camouflaged 3.7cm Pak gun in attack position in the shadow of a KV heavy tank. The technical manual for the antitank gun said that the Soviet heavy tanks could not be destroyed. It was supposed to be possible to put the tank out of commission with a few well-aimed shots into the optics or the drive sprockets.

Immediately taking control of the railway station, a StuG assault gun unit enters a town. The vehicle in the front is an Ausf. B, the other an Ausf. C or D. While supporting infantry, which was what the StuG was originally designed to do, the assault guns decided many battles.

A mixed column of tanks and halftracks advances up a road. The Pz.Kpfw. III in the foreground is from an early Ausf. J producton lot, as is evident by the ball-mounted MG 34 in the front of the hull. The Ausf. J featured many improvements, such as thicker armor on the superstructure, that were made based on combat experience.

Photographed while entering a village, these Pz.Kpfw. IIIs of 11.Panzer-Division each carry a squad of infantrymen. Although it was dangerous for the troops to ride this way since tanks attract enemy fire, this tactic was essential for close combat defense of the tank. They were often threatened by antitank teams, particularly in areas where there were a lot of buildings.

German military transport vehicles suffered badly from the lack of a roadway system in Russia. Here a former civilian-model Mercedes-Benz truck with non-military wheels gets a push from a group of soldiers and civilians after getting stuck on a slippery road. Even a couple of farmer wives are lending a hand to move the vehicle, which belongs to the 1st company, Transport Rgt. 505. Of interest is the variety of tactical markings on the truck.

A StuG III Ausf. B slowly approaches a farmhouse. In general, the assault guns were well-suited for surprise attacks, aided by thick armor and a low silhouette. Concealed antitank teams, however, had to be fought by accompanying infantry. Thus, maximum cooperation was essential. Note the early-style smoke candle rack.

A tank convoy forces its way through deep mud somewhere in Russia. The Pz.Kpfw. III at center, probably an Ausf. J, has its towing cables fitted on the loops and ready for action. All too often the tanks had to stop to recover less maneuverable trucks.

The Germans were highly impressed by the sophisticated Soviet armor. Here a captured KV-1 Model 1940 is displayed for members of a Portuguese military delegation visiting the Leningrad Front in late 1941.

Up until 1941, German tank maintenance units were situated mainly in towns or cities, where large buildings were available. The situation was different in Russia, however. The centralized system was no longer practical, so mobile workshops were established. Here a Pz.Kpfw. III Ausf. G is about to undergo repairs.

This photo, which was taken at a mobile field workshop, shows the complete hull and turret of a Pz.Kpfw. III Ausf. G that were removed using a portable jib. Now that entry to the hull was provided, almost any repair could be made without problems. It is interesting to compare the national insgnia on this hull (with its black interior) with the solid white crosses painted on the tanks in the Polish campaign.

A medium artillery tractor, a Sd.Kfz. 7 8-ton halftrack, tows a 15cm sFH 18 gun across a ditch. The halftracks proved to be excellent prime movers — reliable off the roads and fast on the roads. However, the engineering involved in their production was too complicated and expensive for the war of attrition being carried out in the East.

A Kfz. 69 "Horch" kicks up a cloud of dust as it travels at high speed over some barren Russian countryside. The heavy passenger car is manned by seven soldiers. Of interest is the antiaircraft MG34 fitted in the center of the car and the prominent German cross on the vehicle´s side. Note also the *Wehrmacht Heere*— Wehrmacht Army — license plate prefix.

The Pz.Kpfw. III had to carry the burden of armored warfare in Russia in 1941/42. Basically, it was a well-balanced tank. But with appearance of the superior T-34 and KV, it quickly became obsolete. In this photo, an Ausf. J moves slowly up to the MLR while the commander carefully watches the horizon through his open hatch. The large turret number, "412", indicates that this is the second tank of the first platoon of the fourth company of whatever regiment it belongs to.

This photograph provides an excellent view of an 8.8cm Flak 18 gun in position and ready to go into action. The "88" was able to destroy any Soviet vehicle at ranges far beyond 2,000m (2,200 yards). Thus, it quickly became legendary among the German soldiers — and no doubt among the Russians, as well.

A Pz.Kpfw. III (background) encounters two derelict KV-1 heavy tanks. The strong armor of the Soviet adversary made it almost impossible for German tanks to destroy them. Some reports speak of 40 to 50 direct hits by 37mm and 50mm shells simply bouncing off some KVs. Only heavy antiaircraft guns were able to deal with them.

Stunned motorcyclists pass a similar scene of destruction. The German troops had invaded Russia with the deep conviction that the Blitzkrieg into the East would be concluded in short order, and evidence of German victories like this seemed to support that sentiment. However, as time passed and as Russian resistance stiffened, their optimism waned.

Captured Soviet 76mm field guns were immediately pressed into German service. The German industry inserted a new bore to fire their own 7.5cm ammunition. Called *"Ratschbumm"* for the noise the high velocity round made when it was fired, this gun was formidable in every respect.

This Sd.Kfz. 10/4 shows a partly armored driver´s cabin. These versatile vehicles were often used near the MLR for direct fire support for infantry units, a task they were not intended for. The inadequate armor protection resulted in heavy losses. Note the heavy winter clothing worn by the soldiers.

A convoy of trucks tries with much difficulty to cross a stream. Some of the smaller vehicles apparently broke down, a problem that was typical of such operations. With winter approaching and the Russians showing no sign of weakening their resolve to defend their homeland, the German Army would soon find itself in a tactical quagmire that is foreshadowed by this scene.

Perfectly concealed under some straw, this StuG III waits for action. After the StuG's smaller infantry support gun was replaced with a longer gun, the assault vehicle was a deadly threat to the heavy Russian tanks. Judging from the drive sprocket, this StuG III is an Ausf. B model.

A convoy of Pz.Kpfw. 38(t) tanks passes a column of support vehicles on a snow-covered road. The early winter of 1941 came as a shock to the Germans. The troops were not prepared for the extreme conditions of the Russian winter; many of them even lacked cold-weather clothing.

In 1941 the antitank units equipped with the rare 5cm Pak 38 were fortunate indeed. Although it boasted a sophisticated design, its caliber proved to be too small to deal with modern Soviet armor. However, at ranges below 500m (550 yards), the gun could be quite effective.

Here the crew of a whitewashed StuG III Ausf. E changes the track, possibly because of damage inflicted by a mine. Note that the vehicle was given the name "Leopard", a practice that was common among assault gun units. The vehicle is loaded with a lot of personal gear and spare parts.

Another assault gun of the same unit undergoes the same track replacement procedure. This vehicle, an Ausf. C or D, was named "*Tigerhai*" (Tigershark). Note how the whitewash covers the original paint on every part of the vehicle, but leaves the name visible.

This whitewashed Pz.Kpfw. III Ausf. J encounters Russian peasants escaping from the front line. Although it was planned that the Ausf. J would be equipped with the 5cm L/60 gun, production delays prevented this from happening. So, the first production batches left the factories with the less powerful 5cm L/42 gun. This tank sports a rather scruffy winter camouflage.

The victorious crew of this Pz.Kpfw. III Ausf. J takes a closer look at the T-34 Model 1941 they destroyed. Looting enemy vehicles was a common practice since the supply of clothes and food was never sufficient. The German tank commander shown here wears an improvised winter overcoat that is typical for the first winter.

These assault guns, StuG III Ausf. Es that belong to an unidentified unit, were photographed in the spring of 1942. The winter whitewash, which had been so useful only weeks earlier, was now a problem; the white vehicles were easy to detect from a great distance. The halftrack in the background is a Sd.Kfz. 252 light armored ammunition carrier.

Panzer troops dig out a Pz.Kpfw. III Ausf. J that has been buried by snow. The vehicle, which belongs to 5.Panzer-Division, has suffered just one of the problems of winter warfare. The German advance was successfully stopped by "General Winter"; the front lines could be held only with extreme difficulty. This photo was taken in the beginning of 1942.